Introduction: A Wake-Up Call

I met him in Villa 952. His name doesn't matter because it's not his name that's stayed with me, but his story—and the regret etched into his face. He was in his early 70s, sitting on the patio of the retirement villa, nursing a cup of tea that had long gone cold. His frail body sagged in the chair as if life had drained him one disappointment at a time. He told me how he had worked tirelessly for decades, saving every dollar, deferring every dream, all for this: the golden years he'd been promised. But the golden years never came.

"You think you have time," he said, staring out at the manicured lawn. "You think you'll climb the mountain, reach the summit, and finally enjoy the view. But when you get there, you're too tired to see it."

His words landed like a punch to the gut. He had waited for a someday that never arrived. Health issues crept in during his late 60s, limiting his mobility. Friends he'd planned to travel with were gone. The love of his life, his wife of 40 years, passed away six months before their dream cruise to Greece. "If I could go back to my 50s," he said, voice trembling, "I'd spend it all. The money, the time, the energy. I'd live so big I wouldn't need these golden years."

That conversation changed me. It became a lens through which I started to see everything differently. Life's fragility was no longer an abstract concept but a visceral reality. And I realized how many of us—myself included—are guilty of the same mistake. We've been sold this flawed narrative about life: grind through your youth and middle years, sock away savings, delay gratification, and then—when you've earned it—you can finally start living.

But what if that narrative is a lie?

The Problem: We've Been Sold a Broken Map

We live in a society obsessed with deferred happiness. From the moment we start our first job, we're taught to play the long game. Save for retirement. Build your 401(k) or Superannuation. Plan for later. The idea isn't inherently bad—prudence has its place—but somewhere along the way, it became the *only* way.

We put off the vacations because work is too demanding. We skip out on learning Spanish because it feels frivolous. We hesitate to buy the boat, take the dance lessons, or write the novel because it doesn't fit into the carefully constructed narrative of "later." The cruel irony? Later is never guaranteed.

By the time you reach your late 60s or 70s, the reality of aging often sets in. Your knees don't work like they used to. Your energy flags. The spontaneity that once defined your younger self feels like a distant memory. And worst of all, the person you thought you'd finally have time to become? They feel like a stranger.

It's not just about health, though that's a significant part of it. It's about the mental and emotional toll of waiting too long to live. The longer you defer your dreams, the harder it becomes to even recognize them when they're staring you in the face.

The Wake-Up Call

Not long after my conversation with the man from Villa 952, my own wake-up call arrived in a much more personal way. My father passed away unexpectedly at the age of 62. He had just retired six months earlier, after spending over four decades working long hours at a job that drained him. His plan was to "finally relax."

Except he never got the chance.

In the weeks following his death, I kept finding scraps of paper he'd tucked away in drawers and notebooks—lists of things he wanted to do. Trips he'd planned. Books he wanted to read. Recipes he wanted to try. All of it undone.

One list, in particular, haunts me. It was titled "For My Retirement." It included dreams so modest they made my chest ache—"Visit the Grand Canyon," "Take a pottery class," "Try making homemade pasta." These weren't extravagant bucket list items; they were simple acts of joy, the kind anyone might take for granted. And he'd waited too long for every single one.

The Invitation: This Midlife is Not a Crisis—It's a Call to Action

Here's the truth: midlife is not a crisis. It's a crossroads.

Somewhere in your 50s, something shifts. You've lived long enough to see the fragility of life up close. You've lost people you love. Maybe you've faced your own health scares or started to feel the creeping limitations of time. If you're paying attention, you realize that the "someday" you've been waiting for might not come.

And that realization? It's not a tragedy. It's a gift.

This book is an invitation to wake up to the life you have *now*. Not in your 70s. Not when the mortgage is paid off or the kids are out of the house or the stars align. Now.

Living fully doesn't mean blowing your savings on a whim or throwing caution to the wind. It means rethinking your priorities. It means putting joy, connection, and meaning at the forefront of your life instead of treating them like afterthoughts. It means asking yourself, "What do I want my 50s and 60s to look like?" and having the courage to act on the answer.

You don't have to climb Mount Everest or quit your job to live boldly. It might mean finally taking that art class, learning how to surf, or booking a flight to Italy. It might mean spending more time with your grandchildren, starting a garden, or saying no to work events that drain you. It might mean looking at your bank account and reallocating funds—not toward the nebulous future, but toward the things that light you up right now.

What's Ahead

In the chapters ahead, we're going to explore what it means to live fully in midlife and beyond. We'll talk about redefining your relationship with time, money, health, and relationships. You'll learn how to create a "living budget" that prioritizes joy, how to rediscover your vitality through small daily habits, and how to design a life you love without waiting for permission.

You'll also find exercises and prompts to help you turn ideas into action—because this book isn't just about inspiration; it's about transformation.

If you've ever felt the pull to live more boldly but weren't sure where to start, you're in the right place. If you've ever found yourself saying, "I'll get to it someday," let this book be your nudge to make someday *now*.

This isn't a crisis—it's your renaissance. Welcome to midlife. Let's make it extraordinary.

Chapter 1: The New Midlife

The term *midlife crisis* conjures images of desperation: a gray-haired man trading his minivan for a cherry-red convertible, or a newly divorced woman lighting sage and booking a one-way ticket to Bali in search of herself. For decades, this cliché has been the narrative we've swallowed—that midlife is something to dread, a descent into irrelevance marked by existential angst and dwindling vitality.

But what if the so-called midlife crisis isn't a crisis at all? What if it's an awakening?

Midlife isn't a breakdown; it's a break-open. It's the moment when life holds up a mirror and asks, *Are you really living, or are you just existing?* It's not comfortable—awakening rarely is—but it's transformative. For the first time, you're face-to-face with your own impermanence, and you have a choice: retreat into fear, or lean into freedom.

Debunking the Myth of the Midlife Crisis

The idea of the midlife crisis was born in the 1960s, when psychologist Elliott Jaques coined the term to describe the existential reckoning many people face in their 40s and 50s. But what started as a valid psychological observation was hijacked by pop culture, turning it into a caricature.

In reality, most people don't spiral into chaos at midlife. They evolve. They shed skins. They start asking questions that matter:

- *What do I really want?*
- *Who am I, outside of my job, my marriage, or my role as a parent?*
- *What will I regret if I don't do it now?*

These questions can feel unsettling, but they're also invitations to step into a fuller version of yourself.

The so-called crisis isn't a crisis; it's a shift in perspective. You stop measuring your life by what you've achieved and start focusing on what makes you feel alive. This isn't the beginning of the end—it's the beginning of the beginning.

Midlife as a Renaissance

If youth is about potential, midlife is about possibility.

In your 50s, you've been through enough to know what matters and what doesn't. You've weathered storms, survived heartbreaks, and worn more hats than you ever thought possible. By now, you've let go of the illusion that life is linear. You understand it's a mosaic—a kaleidoscope of moments, choices, and second chances.

This is your renaissance.

Like a phoenix rising, midlife invites you to burn away the parts of your identity that no longer serve you. The corporate ladder-climber, the over-scheduled parent, the people-pleaser—those roles may have defined your first act, but they don't have to define your second.

Think of your 50s as an uncharted horizon. You're no longer tethered to the same expectations or constraints. For many, the kids are grown, the mortgage is manageable, and the career ambitions that once consumed you have loosened their grip. What remains is possibility—the freedom to create, explore, and reinvent.

Reinvention doesn't mean abandoning everything you've built. It means carrying the wisdom of your past into the adventure of your future. It's about trading "What will people think?" for "What do I want?"

A New Generation of Rule Breakers

Statistics paint an inspiring picture of what's possible in midlife and beyond. In the past, hitting 50 was seen as the twilight years—a time to slow down, wind up your career, and ease into retirement. Not anymore.

- **New Careers:** According to a study by the American Institute for Economic Research, 82% of people aged 47 to 60 who made career changes reported feeling successful in their new roles. Whether it's launching a consulting business, diving into freelance work, or finally pursuing that dream of opening a bakery, midlife is fertile ground for professional reinvention.
- **Travel and Exploration:** AARP reports that adults aged 50+ account for 50% of all travel spending in the U.S., with an increasing number of people choosing solo adventures or "gap years" to explore the world.
- **Redefining Aging:** Forget the stereotypes. The over-50 crowd is running marathons, starting nonprofits, and dominating yoga classes. In fact, the Global Wellness Institute notes that wellness tourism among older adults is skyrocketing, as people prioritize health and adventure over passivity.

This isn't your grandparents' midlife. This is a generation rewriting the rules. They're learning to tango, summiting mountains, and running businesses from beachside cabanas. They're proving that it's never too late to live boldly.

What Holds Us Back?

If midlife offers so much potential, why do so many people stay stuck?

The answer often lies in fear. Fear of judgment, fear of failure, fear of the unknown. For decades, you've been conditioned to play it safe. Take the stable job. Save for retirement. Stay in your lane. But the truth is, staying in your lane only works if you're on a road you actually want to travel.

It's not just fear—it's inertia. We fall into routines, roles, and ruts that feel too entrenched to escape. But here's the secret: the hardest part of reinvention isn't the doing—it's the deciding. Once you decide to embrace the possibilities of midlife, the rest is just logistics.

The Stories We Tell Ourselves

One of the greatest obstacles to embracing midlife as a renaissance is the story you tell yourself about what's possible.

- "I'm too old to start over."
- "I don't have the time or energy."
- "People will think I've lost my mind."

These stories are lies. And like any lie, they lose their power when you shine a light on them.

For every excuse, there's a counterexample:

- Julia Child didn't publish her first cookbook until she was 50.
- Vera Wang started designing wedding dresses at 40.

- Harland Sanders (better known as Colonel Sanders) franchised KFC at 62.

The lesson? It's never too late to start something new.

Making the Shift: From Linear to Expansive

In your younger years, life feels linear: graduate, get a job, start a family, climb the ladder, retire. But midlife invites you to step off the treadmill and embrace a more expansive view. Life isn't a straight line; it's a series of chapters, each with its own flavor and purpose.

What if your 50s were the chapter where you finally prioritized joy?

Interactive Element: Rewriting Your Next Chapter

Take a moment to reflect. Imagine your life as a book, and you've just finished writing the first half. What would you want the next chapter to look like?

Journal Prompt:

- If you could rewrite your life's next chapter, what would it include?
    - What passions or hobbies would you explore?
    - What relationships would you nurture or let go of?
    - What places would you visit?
    - What legacy would you start building today?

The New Midlife: A Philosophy of Bold Living

The shift from seeing midlife as a crisis to embracing it as a renaissance isn't just a mental exercise—it's a call to action. It's a challenge to stop deferring your joy and start creating it.

Your 50s and beyond can be the most vibrant, exciting, and meaningful years of your life—if you're willing to let them be. It starts with asking yourself one simple question: *What do I want my life to feel like?*

Midlife isn't the end. It's the start of something extraordinary. And you're just getting started.

Chapter 2: Time is Finite

Time. It's the one thing we all think we have enough of—until suddenly, we don't. We waste it, spend it, try to save it, and sometimes even kill it. But the truth is, time isn't a commodity. It's the air we breathe, the heartbeat of our existence, and it's disappearing faster than most of us are willing to admit.

Let's start with the maths. If you're 50 years old today and fortunate enough to live to 80, you've got 30 years ahead of you. That sounds like plenty, right? Now, strip it down. That's 360 months. If you love celebrating Christmas, you've got about 30 left. Summer vacations? Maybe 30 more beach trips. Family reunions, lazy Sunday brunches, mornings when you wake up without an alarm—those moments, those tiny slivers of joy? They're numbered.

The thought isn't meant to depress you; it's meant to wake you up. Life is finite, but most of us live like it's infinite, pushing our dreams to a future that's not promised. The clock is ticking, and it's asking one question: *What are you going to do with the time you have left?*

The Brevity of Life

The ancient Stoics had a practice called *memento mori*, which translates to "remember that you will die." It wasn't a morbid obsession but a tool for clarity. When you're constantly aware that your time is limited, your priorities have a way of snapping into focus.

Modern science backs this up. Psychologists who study aging and happiness have found that as people grow older, they tend to shift their attention toward the things that truly matter: relationships, meaningful experiences, and personal growth. Why? Because the illusion of endless time fades, and what's left is the urgency to live fully.

Here's a thought experiment: imagine you have five years left. Just five.

- Would you still be putting off that trip to Tuscany?
- Would you still be waiting for "the perfect time" to switch careers, start painting, or learn the guitar?
- Would you still spend your days scrolling through social media, waiting for something exciting to happen to you instead of making it happen yourself?

Common Regrets: The Stories We Carry

Bronnie Ware, a palliative care nurse, wrote a book called *The Top Five Regrets of the Dying*. Over years of sitting with patients in their final days, she began to notice patterns in their reflections. The regrets weren't about things people had done, but about the things they hadn't done.

The top regrets included:

1. **"I wish I'd had the courage to live a life true to myself, not the life others expected of me."**
    - How much of your life has been shaped by other people's expectations? The career path your parents nudged you toward? The relationships you stayed in out of obligation? The dreams you abandoned because they seemed impractica?
2. **"I wish I hadn't worked so hard."**
    - Ware observed that this regret was almost universal among men, but it's increasingly common for women, too. So many people sacrifice their best years on the altar of productivity, only to realize too late that their kids, their partners, and their own passions were the real treasures.
3. **"I wish I'd stayed in touch with my friends."**
    - As we grow older, it's easy to let friendships slip through the cracks. But at the end of life, it's the connections we've built—not the titles we've earned—that bring us the most comfort.
4. **"I wish I'd let myself be happier."**
    - This one always stops me in my tracks. Happiness, as it turns out, is often a choice—a decision to stop chasing perfection and start embracing the beauty of imperfection.

These regrets aren't unique to the dying; they're warnings for the living. They're whispers from those who've reached the end of the road, urging us to change course before it's too late.

The Reality of Aging

Here's the thing about time: it's not just about how many years you have left—it's about how many *good* years you have left.

By your 50s, you've probably noticed some changes. Maybe your knees protest when you stand up too quickly, or your energy isn't quite what it used to be. These aren't signs that life is over—they're reminders to use the energy you have wisely.

- **Health Wanes Over Time:** The Centers for Disease Control (CDC) reports that chronic illnesses like heart disease, diabetes, and arthritis become increasingly common after age 60. Mobility and strength decline, and recovery from injuries takes longer.
- **Energy Shifts:** It's not just physical health—mental and emotional energy evolve, too. You might find yourself less willing to tolerate toxic relationships or soul-sucking jobs, which is a blessing in disguise.

This isn't fear-mongering; it's reality. And the reality is this: the decade you're in right now—your 50s—is a window of opportunity. You're old enough to have wisdom but young enough to still take risks. If you don't seize this time, you're gambling that your 60s or 70s will offer the same opportunities. They might not.

Turning Fear into Action

The finite nature of life isn't something to fear—it's something to leverage. When you know the clock is ticking, you stop wasting time on trivialities. You stop chasing status symbols and start chasing sunsets.

This shift is about living with urgency, not panic. It's about asking yourself, *If not now, when?* and realizing there's no good reason to wait.

Consider this: the average person spends 90,000 hours at work over a lifetime. Ninety. Thousand. Hours. If you're going to give that much of your life to a job, shouldn't it at least be something that fills you up instead of draining you dry?

The same goes for your relationships, your hobbies, your daily routines. Time is your most precious resource, and it's non-refundable.

Interactive Element: Create Your Life Timeline

Let's make this real. Grab a piece of paper or open a blank document, and map out your "Life Timeline."

1. **Start with Today:** Write your current age at the far-left side of the page.
2. **Plot Your Milestones:** Add the ages you hope to reach key milestones. This could include personal goals (traveling to Japan, writing a book), family moments (watching your grandkids graduate), or health aspirations (running a 10K, mastering yoga).
3. **Work Backwards:** Look at the years you have between now and your next milestone. What can

you do this year, this month, or even this week to move closer to that goal?
4. **Mark the "Non-Negotiables":** Highlight the experiences that matter most to you. Maybe it's an annual vacation with your partner, or weekly dinners with your kids. Build your life around these moments.
5. **Reflect:** Ask yourself: *Am I living in a way that honors the time I have left?*

A Call to Live Fully

Time is finite, but that's what makes it precious. The fleeting nature of life isn't something to lament—it's something to cherish.

Every day, you have a choice: to let time slip through your fingers, or to grab it with both hands and make it count. You can keep waiting for "someday," or you can start now. Go after what sets your soul on fire. Spend time with the people who matter most. Say yes to the experiences you've been putting off.

Remember, the clock is ticking—but it's not too late. Your best years aren't behind you; they're ahead, waiting for you to claim them.

So, what will you do with the time you have left?

Chapter 3: Spending Wisely, Living Boldly

Money. We spend our lives chasing it, saving it, and worrying about it, but when was the last time you asked yourself what your money is *for*?

For most of us, the answer has been programmed into us since childhood: security. We've been taught to think of money as a fortress, a shield against the uncertainties of the future. And while there's wisdom in planning for the unexpected, there's also a quiet danger in treating money as the endgame instead of the tool it's meant to be.

If you're reading this, chances are you've spent decades working, budgeting, and saving. You've checked the boxes, done the math, and played it safe. But let me ask you: *When was the last time you spent money on something that truly made you feel alive?*

Confronting Financial Fears

The fear of running out of money is one of the most pervasive anxieties of midlife. It's a whisper that follows you into every decision: *What if I don't have enough?* It's why we skip the trip to Tuscany, put off buying the kayak, and settle for staycations instead of adventures.

But let's take a closer look at this fear. Financial planners have a term called the "spending smile." It's a concept that shows how people's spending changes over the course of their lives. Spending peaks in your 40s and 50s—mortgages, college tuition, family expenses—and then it slowly declines as you age. By the time most people reach their 70s and 80s, their spending is at its lowest point. Why? Because life slows down. Health issues limit travel. Energy wanes. The desire for new experiences diminishes.

This is why hoarding money for your 80s while depriving yourself in your 50s and 60s is such a tragic miscalculation. You're saving for a chapter of life when your ability to enjoy it is significantly reduced. What if, instead, you shifted your focus to spending intentionally—while you still have the energy and vitality to make the most of it?

The question isn't *"Will I run out of money?"* The question is *"Am I using my money to live the life I want today?"*

The Living Budget

Let's reframe the way we think about money. Instead of a fortress, imagine your finances as a canvas. Every dollar is a brushstroke, and the masterpiece you're painting is your life.

This is where the concept of a "Living Budget" comes in. A Living Budget isn't about reckless spending or ignoring future needs; it's about aligning your financial decisions with your values and priorities. It's about funding a life that feels rich in experiences, relationships, and personal growth—not just in dollars and cents.

How to Create a Living Budget

1. **Start with Your Essentials**
   First, cover your basics: housing, food, healthcare, and anything else that keeps the lights on and the bills paid. This is your foundation.
2. **Define Your Priorities**
   Take a moment to reflect: What brings you the most joy? Is it travel? Learning a new skill? Spending time with family? Write down the top three things that make your life feel meaningful. These are the pillars of your Living Budget.
3. **Allocate Funds for Joy**
   Look at your budget and allocate a specific percentage of your income toward experiences that light you up. This might be 10%, 20%, or whatever feels right for your financial situation. The key is to make this a *priority*, not an afterthought.
4. **Revisit and Adjust**
   Life changes, and so do your needs. Revisit your Living Budget every six months to make sure it still aligns with your goals.

An Example

Let's say you earn $80,000 a year. After covering essentials (let's estimate $50,000), you have $30,000 left.

- You might allocate $10,000 for travel, $5,000 for hobbies or classes, and $2,000 for family experiences like a reunion or special celebration.
- The rest can go into long-term savings, but the point is to *spend intentionally* on the things that bring you joy now.

Reframing Wealth: It's About Meaning, Not Accumulation

Wealth, in its truest sense, has never been about the numbers in your bank account. It's about the life those numbers can create.

Think of the people you admire most. Chances are, their impact wasn't defined by their net worth but by the richness of their lives—the stories they told, the risks they took, the relationships they nurtured.

There's a famous story about the late chef and writer Anthony Bourdain. At the height of his career, he was traveling 200 days a year, eating at some of the world's best restaurants. A journalist once asked him, "What are you saving for?" Bourdain shrugged and said, "Nothing. I just want to have a good story to tell."

That's wealth. Not the accumulation of things, but the accumulation of meaning.

When you reframe wealth as a tool for living, the question shifts from *"How much can I save?"* to *"How can I use what I have to create a life I love?"*

Practical Tips for Bold Spending

1. Invest in Experiences, Not Things

Studies show that people derive more happiness from experiences than from material possessions. Why? Because experiences create memories, deepen connections, and give you stories to share.

2. Share Your Wealth

Some of life's greatest joys come from generosity. Whether it's treating a friend to dinner, funding a grandchild's education, or donating to a cause you believe in, sharing your wealth is one of the most meaningful ways to spend it.

3. Spend on Health and Well-Being

Think of money spent on your health—gym memberships, yoga classes, nutritious food—as an investment in your future. The healthier you are, the more fully you can enjoy your life.

4. Plan for Spontaneity

Set aside a small "spontaneity fund" for those unplanned moments that bring joy. Maybe it's a last-minute weekend getaway or tickets to a concert you hadn't budgeted for. The point is to say yes when life surprises you.

Interactive Element: Your Living Budget

Take a moment to sit with your financial reality—not in fear, but in curiosity. Let's build your Living Budget:

1. **Start with a blank page or spreadsheet.**
2. **List your essentials.** Write down your fixed expenses: mortgage, utilities, food, insurance, etc. Subtract this total from your income.
3. **Prioritize joy.** From the remaining amount, allocate funds to the things that matter most to you—travel, hobbies, family, learning. Be specific.
4. **Leave room for savings.** Allocate a portion for long-term needs, but resist the urge to hoard. Balance is key.
5. **Name one thing you'll do this year with your budget.**

Journal Prompt: If Money Were No Obstacle

Ask yourself: *If money were no obstacle, what would you do this year?*

- Would you travel?
- Start a passion project?
- Learn a new skill?
  Write it down, and then ask: *What's stopping me?*

The Courage to Spend Boldly

Spending wisely and living boldly aren't opposites—they're two sides of the same coin. When you spend with intention, your money becomes a vehicle for creating the life you want, not a prison that keeps you from it.

So, buy the ticket. Take the class. Host the party. The fortune you've built—whether it's big or small—isn't just for surviving. It's for thriving.

Life is short, but it's also beautiful. And the best stories don't come from the things we save—they come from the moments we spend.

Chapter 4: Rediscovering Vitality

There's a moment for all of us when our bodies remind us we're not 25 anymore. Maybe it's the twinge in your knee after climbing the stairs, or the way a second glass of wine hits harder than it used to. For some, it's more serious—a diagnosis, an injury, a health scare that stops you in your tracks.

And here's the thing: it's tempting to view these moments as the beginning of the end, a sign that life is inevitably winding down. But they can also be something else entirely. They can be the wake-up call you didn't know you needed—a reminder that your body isn't a machine; it's a living, breathing companion on this journey.

The good news? It's never too late to start taking better care of it.

Vitality Isn't Youth—It's Energy in the Present Moment

Let's get one thing straight: vitality isn't about trying to recapture your 20s. It's not about six-pack abs, running marathons, or chasing the fountain of youth. It's about energy—having enough of it to do the things you love, to show up for the people who matter, and to feel alive in your own skin.

Vitality isn't about looking younger; it's about feeling better. And the path to rediscovering it isn't paved with crash diets or punishing workouts. It's about small, sustainable habits that honor the body you have today.

Physical Health: Building a Stronger Foundation

1. Move Daily, But Move Smart

You don't need to run triathlons to stay fit in your 50s and 60s. In fact, the most impactful exercise is often the simplest. Walking, for instance, is a near-perfect form of movement. It's gentle on your joints, improves cardiovascular health, and clears your mind in a way few other activities can.

If you want to take it a step further, consider strength training. Studies show that after age 50, we lose muscle mass at an accelerating rate—about 1% per year. Lifting weights, even light ones, can reverse this trend, improving bone density, balance, and overall vitality.

How to Start:

- Walk for 30 minutes a day. If that feels like too much, start with 10 and build up.
- Incorporate strength training twice a week. Bodyweight exercises like squats, lunges, and push-ups are a great place to begin.

2. Eat Like Your Life Depends On It

Because it does.

Nutrition in midlife isn't about restriction or fad diets. It's about nourishing your body in a way that supports longevity and energy. The Mediterranean diet—a way of eating rich in fruits, vegetables, whole grains, lean protein, and healthy fats—has been shown to reduce inflammation, boost brain health, and lower the risk of chronic disease.

But it's not just about *what* you eat; it's about *how*. Slow down. Taste your food. Treat meals as an act of self-care, not a chore to rush through.

How to Start:

- Add more plants to your plate—aim for five servings of fruits and vegetables daily.
- Swap processed snacks for whole foods like nuts, yogurt, or fresh fruit.
- Hydrate. Your body is about 60% water, and even mild dehydration can sap your energy.

---

3. Sleep: The Ultimate Reset Button

Sleep is the unsung hero of vitality. It's when your body repairs, your brain consolidates memories, and your energy reserves replenish. Yet many of us treat it like an afterthought, squeezing it in around the edges of our busy lives.

If you're waking up groggy, hitting a mid-afternoon slump, or struggling to fall asleep, it's time to rethink your sleep hygiene.

How to Start:

- Set a consistent bedtime and wake time, even on weekends.
- Create a calming pre-sleep ritual: dim the lights, read a book, or practice deep breathing.
- Avoid screens for at least an hour before bed—the blue light can disrupt your melatonin production.

Mental Health: Tending to Your Inner World

Rediscovering vitality isn't just about the body; it's about the mind. Stress, anxiety, and emotional baggage can sap your energy just as much as poor nutrition or lack of exercise. The solution? Cultivating practices that nurture your mental well-being.

1. Mindfulness: The Art of Being Here Now

Ram Dass said it best: *"Be here now."*

Mindfulness isn't about sitting cross-legged on a mountaintop; it's about paying attention to the present moment without judgment. It's a practice that can reduce stress, improve focus, and increase your capacity for joy.

Start small. Five minutes a day is enough to feel the benefits.

How to Start:

- Find a quiet place. Sit comfortably and focus on your breath.

- When your mind wanders (and it will), gently bring it back to your breath.
- Apps like Headspace or Calm can guide you if you're new to meditation.

2. Stress Management: Lightening the Load

Stress is inevitable, but it doesn't have to rule your life. The key is learning to respond to it in a healthier way. Exercise, mindfulness, and creative outlets like writing or painting can all help. So can saying no to commitments that drain you.

How to Start:

- Identify your biggest stressors and brainstorm ways to minimize or manage them.
- Practice gratitude. Studies show that focusing on what you're thankful for can reduce stress and boost happiness.

3. Connection: You're Not Meant to Do This Alone

Human connection is a powerful antidote to stress and a key ingredient for vitality. Whether it's a deep conversation with a friend, a shared laugh with family, or even a moment of kindness with a stranger, connection fuels the soul.

Make it a priority.

How to Start:

- Schedule regular phone calls or coffee dates with loved ones.
- Join a community group, class, or volunteer organization to meet like-minded people.

Energy Boosters: Simple Tips to Stay Charged

1. **Move Every Hour:** If you're sitting for long stretches, stand up, stretch, or take a quick walk.
2. **Eat Smaller, Balanced Meals:** Avoid the energy crashes that come with heavy, carb-loaded lunches.
3. **Take Micro-Breaks:** Even five minutes of deep breathing or a quick walk around the block can reset your energy.
4. **Surround Yourself with Positivity:** Spend time with people who uplift you and limit exposure to those who drain you.

Interactive Element: The Vitality Tracker

Building new habits takes consistency. Use this simple weekly chart to track your progress:

Day	Walk (minutes)	Strength Training	Mindfulness (minutes)	Water Intake (glasses)	Sleep Hours
Monday					
Tuesday					
Wednesday					
Thursday					
Friday					
Saturday					
Sunday					

At the end of each week, reflect: *What worked? What could I improve?*

Interactive Element: The Vitality Tracker

Building new habits takes consistency. Use this simple weekly chart to track your progress:

Rediscovering Vitality Is a Journey, Not a Destination

Vitality isn't about perfection; it's about progress. It's about waking up each day with a little more energy, a little more clarity, and a little more joy.

The path is simple but not always easy. It requires showing up for yourself in small ways, day after day. But here's the reward: when you nurture your body and mind, they'll repay you with the energy to live the life you've been dreaming of.

So take the walk. Lift the weights. Breathe deeply. The journey to rediscovering vitality starts right here, right now.

Chapter 5: Relationships Matter Most

It doesn't matter how many miles you've traveled, how many zeros are in your bank account, or how many accolades line your walls. At the end of the day, the question that shapes your life isn't *"What have you achieved?"* It's *"Who have you loved?"*

We're born into this world wired for connection. As infants, we cry for touch. As children, we seek comfort in familiar faces. As adults, we crave intimacy, camaraderie, and belonging. And yet, in the grind of daily life, relationships often become an afterthought. We assume they'll always be there—until, one day, they're not.

When you strip away the noise and distractions, what's left is this simple truth: the people in your life are the greatest source of fulfillment you'll ever know.

The Core of Fulfillment

If you've ever wondered what the secret to happiness is, Harvard may have the answer. The *Harvard Study of Adult Development*, one of the longest-running studies of human life, has been tracking participants for over 80 years. Its conclusion is strikingly simple:

Good relationships keep us healthier and happier. Period.

Not wealth. Not status. Not career success. The quality of your relationships is the most reliable predictor of a long and fulfilling life. Participants with strong social connections not only reported greater happiness but also lived longer, with fewer chronic health issues.

And it's not just Harvard. Psychologist Susan Pinker, in her book *The Village Effect*, highlights research showing that close relationships—whether with family, friends, or community—are as vital to our well-being as food and exercise.

Here's why this matters: in your 50s and beyond, the focus shifts. The career ladder no longer looms so tall. The kids, if you have them, may have flown the nest. You find yourself standing at a crossroads, with time and energy to spend. And the question becomes: *How will I spend it?*

The Cost of Neglecting Relationships

When we fail to nurture our relationships, the consequences are often quiet but profound. Loneliness is a thief—it steals not just joy but also time. Studies show that chronic loneliness can have the same impact on your health as smoking 15 cigarettes a day. It increases your risk of heart disease, depression, and even cognitive decline.

The sad irony is that loneliness often creeps in during midlife, just when we have the most to gain from connection. Careers, obligations, and distractions pull us away from the people who matter most. Friends drift apart. Family ties loosen. Communities fragment.

But here's the good news: it's never too late to reconnect.

Nurturing Bonds: Rebuilding Connection

1. Reconnecting with Family

Family relationships can be some of the most rewarding—and the most complicated. Whether it's a sibling you've lost touch with, a parent who needs more of your time, or a grown child navigating their own life, midlife is the perfect opportunity to bridge gaps.

Practical Tips:

- **Start Small:** Relationships don't have to be repaired in one grand gesture. Sometimes, a simple text or phone call is enough to reignite the connection.
- **Be Present:** When you're with family, put your phone down. Make eye contact. Listen deeply.
- **Let Go of Old Wounds:** This isn't about forgetting, but about choosing peace over resentment.

2. Deepening Friendships

Friends are the family we choose, yet they're often the first to take a backseat when life gets busy. Midlife is a chance to rediscover the joy of friendship—those shared laughs, long talks, and moments of pure understanding.

Practical Tips:

- **Schedule Regular Time:** Whether it's a monthly dinner or a weekly walk, make time for your closest friends.
- **Show Up:** Be the friend who celebrates their wins and supports them through their struggles.
- **Try Something New Together:** Take a cooking class, plan a road trip, or join a group activity to create new shared experiences.

---

3. Cultivating Community

Humans aren't meant to live in isolation. Whether it's a book club, a religious group, a sports league, or a volunteer organization, being part of a community gives you a sense of belonging and purpose.

Practical Tips:

- **Join a Group:** Look for local meetups or online communities that align with your interests.

- **Give Back:** Volunteering is one of the most powerful ways to connect with others while making a difference.
- **Host Gatherings:** Create your own community by hosting dinners, game nights, or neighborhood events.

Legacy Through Connection

When you invest in relationships, you're not just enriching your life—you're creating a ripple effect that extends far beyond you.

Think about the people who've left a mark on your life. Chances are, it wasn't their wealth or accomplishments that stayed with you. It was their kindness, their wisdom, their presence. These are the things that endure, long after we're gone.

Midlife is the perfect time to think about your legacy—not in terms of what you'll leave behind, but in terms of how you'll live now. The memories you create with loved ones, the time you spend nurturing bonds, the love you pour into the world—this is the legacy that truly matters.

Interactive Element: Who Matters Most?

Take a moment to reflect. Grab a notebook or journal and answer the following prompts:

1. Who are the five most important people in your life right now?
2. How often do you spend meaningful time with them?
3. What's one thing you can do this week to strengthen those relationships?

As you write, remember: it's not about perfection. It's about presence.

The Art of Showing Up

Ram Dass once said, *"We're all just walking each other home."* And isn't that what relationships are, at their core? A way of walking through life together, of reminding each other that we're not alone.

In the end, it's not the big gestures that matter most—it's the small, consistent acts of love. The phone call to say, "I'm thinking of you." The hug that lingers a little longer. The shared meal where you laugh until your stomach hurts.

If you do one thing after reading this chapter, let it be this: show up. For your family, your friends, your community—and for yourself. Because in a world that's constantly pulling us apart, choosing connection is the bravest thing you can do.

And when you look back on your life, it won't be the work meetings or the deadlines that you remember. It will be the faces of the people you loved, the stories you shared, and the moments you spent walking each other home.

Chapter 6: Designing a Life You Love

The word "design" usually makes us think of architecture, fashion, or maybe interior decorating. But what if you thought about your life that way? What if, instead of drifting along on autopilot, you took the time to deliberately design a life that feels authentic, joyful, and uniquely yours?

Most of us spend decades in reaction mode—chasing promotions, raising kids, paying bills. It's a life of putting out fires, meeting deadlines, and crossing items off endless to-do lists. Somewhere along the way, we forget that life isn't just about survival. It's about creation. It's about waking up each morning excited about what's ahead.

If you've reached midlife feeling like your spark has dimmed, don't despair. The good news is, you're not out of time. In fact, you're right on time.

Rediscovering Passions

When was the last time you did something purely for the joy of it? Not because it was productive, not because it checked a box, but because it made you feel alive?

For many of us, the answer is buried somewhere in the past. Maybe it was painting in college, hiking on weekends, or playing guitar when the house was quiet. These passions tend to fade into the background when life gets busy. We tell ourselves, *I'll get back to it someday.*

But here's the thing: "someday" doesn't magically appear. You have to claim it.

Midlife is your opportunity to dust off those forgotten passions and make them part of your life again. It's not about being the best painter or hiker or musician; it's about reconnecting with the parts of yourself that bring joy.

Practical Steps to Rediscover Your Passions

1. **Make a List of Joyful Activities**
   - Write down everything that's ever made you feel energized or fulfilled, even if it was years ago. Don't overthink it—just let the ideas flow.
2. **Start Small**
   - If you loved painting but haven't touched a brush in decades, don't pressure yourself to create a masterpiece. Start with a simple sketch or a single color on canvas.
3. **Schedule It**
   - Treat your passion like any other important appointment. Block off time in your calendar, and honor it.

Moving Beyond the Typical Bucket List

The term "bucket list" has become synonymous with skydiving, world travel and other adrenaline-fueled adventures. And while those can be amazing experiences, a meaningful bucket list goes deeper. It's not just about crossing off items; it's about creating a life rich in experiences, relationships, and growth.

Expanding Your Bucket List

- **Personal Growth**
  What skills or knowledge have you always wanted to explore? Maybe it's learning a new language, taking a cooking class, or mastering the art of photography.
- **Creative Pursuits**
  Creativity isn't just for artists—it's for anyone who wants to express themselves. Write a book, compose a song, build furniture, or design a garden. Creativity nourishes the soul.
- **Acts of Service**
  Few things are as fulfilling as giving back. Volunteer at a shelter, mentor a young person, or start a community project. Purpose is amplified when shared with others.
- **Connection Goals**
  Prioritize relationships. Plan a family reunion, take your best friend on a dream trip, or host a monthly dinner with loved ones.
- **Adventure on Your Terms**
  Adventure doesn't have to mean bungee jumping. It could be taking a solo road trip, camping under the stars, or hiking a local trail you've never explored.

How to Create Your Midlife Bucket List

1. **Reflect on What Matters**
   - Ask yourself: *What experiences would I regret not having? What legacy do I want to leave?*
2. **Write It All Down**
   - List everything that sparks excitement, no matter how small or big.
3. **Prioritize**
   - Identify the top five items that resonate most with you and focus on those first.
4. **Set a Timeline**
   - Give yourself realistic but firm deadlines for each goal.

Finding Purpose Beyond Work

For decades, your identity may have been tied to your career. Your business card, your title, your achievements—all markers of success. But what happens when the 9-to-5 no longer defines you?

This transition can feel disorienting, even frightening. But it's also an invitation to redefine your purpose—not in terms of a job, but in terms of what gives your life meaning.

Redefining Success

Success in midlife isn't about climbing ladders; it's about alignment. Are you spending your time in ways that reflect your values? Are you giving your energy to the people and activities that matter most?

Questions to Help You Discover Your Purpose

- *What excites me when I think about the future?*
- *Who do I want to help or inspire?*
- *What causes or issues do I care deeply about?*
- *What would make me proud when I look back on my life?*

Designing Your Days with Intention

If you want to design a life you love, start by designing days you love.

1. **Morning Rituals**
   How you start your day sets the tone for everything else. Incorporate activities that energize and center you—whether it's meditation, journaling, or a brisk walk.
2. **Micro-Joys**
   Sprinkle small moments of joy throughout your day. A favorite song, a cup of tea, a walk in the sun—these moments add up.
3. **Evening Wind-Down**
   End your day with gratitude. Reflect on what went well and set intentions for tomorrow.

Interactive Element: Midlife Bucket List Template

Use the template below to start designing your bucket list.

Category	Goal	Timeline	First Step
Personal Growth	Learn to play the piano	Within 6 months	Find a local teacher or online course
Creative Pursuits	Write a short story	By the end of this year	Set aside 1 hour each week to write
Acts of Service	Volunteer at a food bank	Next month	Research local opportunities
Adventure	Visit the Grand Canyon	Next summer	Book flights and accommodation
Connection Goals	Host a monthly family dinner	Starting this month	Send invitations to loved ones

---

Journal Prompt: What Makes You Lose Track of Time?

Take 10 minutes to journal on the following:

- What activities make you forget to check the clock?
- When do you feel most alive and engaged?
- How can you incorporate more of these moments into your life?

The Courage to Create

Designing a life you love takes courage. It means stepping off the beaten path, letting go of other people's expectations, and daring to ask, *What do I really want?*

But here's the beauty of midlife: you've earned the right to answer that question honestly. You've lived long enough to know what matters and wise enough to know that life isn't about perfection. It's about showing up, taking risks, and savoring the moments that make your heart sing.

So pick up the brush and start painting. The masterpiece of your life is waiting to be created, and the only limit is your imagination.

Chapter 7: The Art of Letting Go

There's a beauty in holding on. To memories, to people, to dreams. But there's an equal beauty—perhaps an even greater one—in knowing when to let go.

Letting go isn't about giving up; it's about making space. Space for the life you've been too busy to notice, for the experiences you've been too burdened to enjoy, and for the freedom you didn't know you could feel.

But here's the thing: letting go isn't something we're taught. Instead, we're raised to believe that more is better—more achievements, more stuff, more status. We cling to identities that no longer serve us, out of fear that without them, we'll be nothing at all.

The truth? Letting go isn't a loss. It's a liberation.

Shedding Societal Expectations

For decades, you've been living according to a script. You know the one:

- Graduate.
- Get a job.
- Climb the ladder.
- Buy the house.
- Raise the kids.
- Save for retirement.

48

It's a script written by society, handed to you before you even knew you had a choice. And while parts of it may have served you well, midlife is the perfect moment to ask: *Whose script am I following?*

Letting go of societal expectations isn't about rejecting everything you've built. It's about questioning what's truly yours. Are you still chasing a career that no longer excites you? Staying in a role—professional or personal—because you think you *should*? Are you clinging to an image of yourself that no longer fits, simply because you're afraid to see what's underneath?

This is your chance to rewrite the script. To stop living for what others expect of you and start living for what feels true to you.

How to Begin:

- **Identify Your "Shoulds":** What are the things you're doing out of obligation, not desire? Write them down.
- **Challenge Them:** Ask yourself, *Is this adding to my life, or is it holding me back?*
- **Choose Freedom:** Let go of the "shoulds" that no longer align with who you are or who you want to be.

Embracing Simplicity

Letting go isn't just about expectations; it's also about stuff. The clutter in your home, the noise in your schedule, the relationships that drain you instead of lifting you up—all of it takes up space that could be used for something better.

1. Materialism: The Weight You Don't Realize You're Carrying

We live in a culture of accumulation. Bigger houses, faster cars, newer gadgets. We're told that happiness is just one purchase away, but deep down, we know that's a lie.

Every item you own demands something from you—time to maintain it, money to store it, mental energy to worry about it. The more you have, the heavier the load.

Letting go of materialism doesn't mean renouncing all possessions. It means keeping only what adds value to your life and releasing the rest.

How to Start:

- **Declutter Your Space:** Choose one area—your closet, your kitchen, your garage. Ask yourself, *Does this item bring me joy or serve a purpose*? If not, let it go.
- **Simplify Your Choices:** Reduce decision fatigue by paring down your wardrobe, meal planning, or streamlining your daily routines.
- **Prioritize Experiences Over Things:** Spend your money on moments, not material goods.

2. Toxic Relationships: The People Who Drain Your Energy

Not everyone in your life is meant to stay. Some relationships lift you up, while others weigh you down. And as painful as it can be, letting go of toxic people is one of the greatest acts of self-love you can offer yourself.

Toxic relationships aren't always obvious. Sometimes, they're marked by manipulation or hostility. Other times, they're simply one-sided, with you giving far more than you receive.

Signs of a Toxic Relationship:

- You feel drained or anxious after spending time with the person.
- They undermine your confidence or belittle your dreams.
- The relationship feels transactional rather than mutual.

How to Let Go:

- **Set Boundaries:** Communicate your needs clearly and enforce limits.
- **Prioritize Healthy Relationships:** Focus your energy on people who uplift and support you.
- **Release with Love:** Letting go doesn't have to be bitter. Wish the person well and move forward.

3. Unnecessary Ambitions: Redefining Success

Midlife is the perfect time to reevaluate what success means to you. Are you chasing goals that genuinely matter, or are you climbing a ladder you no longer care about?

Ambition isn't inherently bad, but unnecessary ambition—pursuing things out of ego, fear, or habit—can rob you of joy. Letting go of these ambitions doesn't mean settling; it means realigning your efforts with your true desires.

Reflection Questions:

- What am I working toward, and why?
- Is this goal bringing me closer to the life I want, or is it pulling me further away?
- What would happen if I let this go?

Cultivating Contentment

Contentment isn't about having it all; it's about appreciating what you have. It's a practice of mindfulness, of being fully present in your life instead of constantly yearning for something else.

Ram Dass once said, *"The quieter you become, the more you can hear."* Letting go creates that quiet. It allows you to hear the whispers of joy in everyday moments—the warmth of the sun on your skin, the laughter of a friend, the simple pleasure of a good meal.

How to Practice Mindfulness

- **Pause Daily:** Take five minutes to simply breathe and notice your surroundings.
- **Focus on Your Senses:** What do you see, hear, feel, smell, and taste right now?
- **Celebrate Small Joys:** Keep a gratitude journal and write down three things you're thankful for each day.

Contentment isn't something you find; it's something you create.

Interactive Element: The Letting Go List

Grab a pen and paper, and create your own "Letting Go" list.

1. **What Expectations Are Weighing You Down?**
   Example: "I need to stay in this job because it looks good on paper."
2. **What Possessions No Longer Serve You?**
   Example: "The closet full of clothes I haven't worn in years."
3. **What Relationships Need Reevaluation?**
   Example: "The friend who always takes but never gives."
4. **What Ambitions Are You Ready to Release?**
   Example: "The idea that I need to prove my worth through achievement."

Commit to letting go of at least one item from your list this week.

The Freedom of Letting Go

Here's the paradox of letting go: the more you release, the more you gain. Letting go of societal expectations gives you freedom. Letting go of material clutter gives you clarity. Letting go of toxic relationships gives you peace.

And letting go of the need for control—the belief that you can hold onto everything forever—gives you the most precious gift of all: presence.

When you stop clinging to what doesn't matter, you create space for what does. And that space? That's where life happens.

So let go. Lighten the load. Trust that what's meant for you will stay, and what's not will make room for something better. Because the art of letting go isn't about losing—it's about finding yourself.

Conclusion: Your Legacy Starts Now

Legacies are funny things. For so long, the word conjures images of grandeur: a name etched into the foundation of a hospital, a sprawling estate passed down through generations, a statue standing solemnly in a park. But here's the thing about those legacies: they're hollow without meaning.

The real legacy isn't in the stuff we leave behind; it's in the way we make people feel, the stories they tell about us, and the echoes of love and kindness that ripple long after we're gone. And you don't need a trust fund or a Pulitzer Prize to leave one. Your legacy starts now—in the choices you make, the moments you create, and the life you decide to live boldly and intentionally.

A Wake-Up Call to Stop Waiting

I met a woman once, sitting at a café in Paris. She must have been in her 80s, her face weathered with stories and her eyes sparkling with mischief. I couldn't resist striking up a conversation—she had the air of someone who knew things the rest of us were still trying to figure out.

We talked about travel, love, and the art of enjoying a good glass of wine. At some point, I asked her, "What's the secret to a life well-lived?"

She leaned in, as if she were about to reveal the most profound truth of the universe. "Stop waiting," she said. "Whatever it is, whoever it is, whatever you dream of—don't wait for someday. Do it now. The clock doesn't stop for anyone."

Her words hung in the air like the perfect note in a jazz song.

Living Fully and Intentionally

If you've made it this far in the book, you already know this truth: life doesn't wait. Not for perfect timing, not for more money, not for the stars to align. Waiting is a luxury we think we can afford, but it's the fastest way to lose the time we have left.

Living fully doesn't mean living recklessly. It's not about throwing caution to the wind or emptying your bank account on a whim. It's about intention—choosing to fill your days with the things that matter most to you. It's about refusing to let fear or inertia keep you from the life you want.

How to Start Living Boldly Today

1. **Say Yes to What Lights You Up**
   If there's something you've been longing to do—write the book, plan the trip, start the business—stop putting it off. Start now, even if it's messy, imperfect, or inconvenient.
2. **Say No to What Drains You**
   Protect your time and energy fiercely. Life is too short to spend on obligations that leave you resentful or unfulfilled.
3. **Embrace Imperfection**
   The perfect moment doesn't exist. If you wait until you're ready, you'll be waiting forever. Start now, and figure it out as you go.
4. **Celebrate the Small Wins**
   Living boldly doesn't have to mean grand gestures. Sometimes, it's the little moments—laughing with a friend, finishing a book, taking a long walk—that remind us how good life can be.

Redefining Your Legacy

For too long, we've been told that legacy is something we leave behind, something to worry about when we're old or gone. But what if legacy isn't about the end of your life? What if it's about how you live today?

Your legacy isn't in the accolades you earn or the stuff you accumulate. It's in the kindness you show, the love you give, and the joy you bring into the world. It's in the way you make your friends laugh, the memories you create with your family, the way you show up for your community.

Think about the people who've left a mark on your life. Chances are, it wasn't their money, titles, or accomplishments that stayed with you. It was the way they made you feel—the way they showed up, the way they cared, the way they lived.

That's the legacy you're creating, whether you realize it or not. And you don't have to wait for someday to start building it.

An Inspiring Reflection

I once read about a hospice nurse who asked her patients, "What do you wish you'd done differently?" The answers were almost never about money, status, or achievements. Instead, they were simple and profound:

- "I wish I'd spent more time with the people I loved."

- "I wish I'd taken more risks."
- "I wish I hadn't worried so much about what others thought."

These aren't regrets of failure; they're regrets of inaction. They're reminders to live while you can, to love while you're able, and to laugh as much as possible along the way.

Interactive Element: Your Legacy Starts Here

Take a moment to reflect on your own life. Grab a notebook or journal and answer these prompts:

1. **What Will You Do This Week to Begin Living Boldly?**
   - Is there a phone call you've been meaning to make? A passion project you've been putting off? A friend you want to reconnect with? Commit to one bold action this week.
2. **What Do You Want People to Remember About You?**
   - How do you want to make people feel? What kind of memories do you want to leave behind?
3. **What's One Small Change You Can Make Today?**
   - It doesn't have to be big. Maybe it's saying thank you more often, smiling at strangers, or taking 10 minutes to meditate.

Final Words: The Journey Begins Now

The beauty of life is that it's constantly unfolding. Every day is a blank page, and you get to decide how to fill it. You don't need permission. You don't need to wait for the right moment. You don't need to do it perfectly.

Start where you are, with what you have. Take the trip. Call the friend. Dance in your living room. Laugh until your stomach hurts. These are the moments that make life worth living.

And remember: your legacy isn't just what you leave behind. It's the life you live right now. So go out there and live boldly, beautifully, and unapologetically.

The clock is ticking, but the story is yours to write. What will you do with the time you have left?

www.ingramcontent.com/pod-product-compliance
Lightning Source LLC
Chambersburg PA
CBHW070958240526
45469CB00017B/2447